TODAY'S DATE: _____

TODAY I AM FEELING:

- ☐ 😊 HAPPY
- ☐ 😐 JUST OKAY
- ☐ ☹️ SAD
- ☐ 😠 MAD

DESCRIBE TODAY:
_____

ONE THING THAT MADE ME HAPPY TODAY:
_____
_____
_____
_____
_____
_____
_____
_____

ONE THING THAT MADE ME SAD OR MAD TODAY:
_____
_____
_____
_____
_____
_____
_____
_____

ONE THING I LEARNED TODAY:
_____
_____
_____
_____

TODAY'S DATE: _____

TODAY I AM FEELING:

- ☐ 😊 HAPPY
- ☐ 😐 JUST OKAY
- ☐ ☹️ SAD
- ☐ 😠 MAD

ONE WORD I WOULD USE TO DESCRIBE TODAY:

_____

ONE THING THAT MADE ME HAPPY TODAY:

_____
_____
_____
_____
_____
_____
_____
_____

ONE THING THAT MADE ME SAD OR MAD TODAY:

_____
_____
_____
_____
_____
_____
_____
_____

ONE THING I LEARNED TODAY:

_____
_____
_____

TODAY'S DATE: _____

TODAY I AM FEELING:
- ☐ 🙂 HAPPY
- ☐ 😐 JUST OKAY
- ☐ 🙁 SAD
- ☐ 😠 MAD

ONE WORD I WOULD USE TO DESCRIBE TODAY:
_____

ONE THING THAT MADE ME HAPPY TODAY:
_____
_____
_____
_____
_____
_____
_____
_____

ONE THING THAT MADE ME SAD OR MAD TODAY:
_____
_____
_____
_____
_____
_____
_____
_____

ONE THING I LEARNED TODAY:
_____
_____
_____

TODAY'S DATE: _____

TODAY I AM FEELING:

- ☐ 🙂 HAPPY
- ☐ 😐 JUST OKAY
- ☐ 🙁 SAD
- ☐ 😠 MAD

ONE WORD I WOULD USE TO DESCRIBE TODAY:

_____

ONE THING THAT MADE ME HAPPY TODAY:

_____
_____
_____
_____
_____
_____
_____
_____

ONE THING THAT MADE ME SAD OR MAD TODAY:

_____
_____
_____
_____
_____
_____
_____
_____

ONE THING I LEARNED TODAY:

_____
_____
_____

TODAY'S DATE: _____

TODAY I AM FEELING:

- ☐ 😊 HAPPY
- ☐ 😐 JUST OKAY
- ☐ 😟 SAD
- ☐ 😠 MAD

ONE WORD I WOULD USE TO DESCRIBE TODAY:

_____

ONE THING THAT MADE ME HAPPY TODAY:

_____
_____
_____
_____
_____
_____
_____
_____

ONE THING THAT MADE ME SAD OR MAD TODAY:

_____
_____
_____
_____
_____
_____
_____
_____

ONE THING I LEARNED TODAY:

_____
_____
_____

TODAY'S DATE: _____

TODAY I AM FEELING:

- [ ] 🙂 HAPPY
- [ ] 😐 JUST OKAY
- [ ] ☹️ SAD
- [ ] 😠 MAD

ONE WORD I WOULD USE TO DESCRIBE TODAY:

_____

ONE THING THAT MADE ME HAPPY TODAY:

_____
_____
_____
_____
_____
_____
_____
_____

ONE THING THAT MADE ME SAD OR MAD TODAY:

_____
_____
_____
_____
_____
_____
_____
_____

ONE THING I LEARNED TODAY:

_____
_____
_____
_____

TODAY'S DATE: _____

TODAY I AM FEELING:

- ☐ 🙂 HAPPY
- ☐ 😐 JUST OKAY
- ☐ 🙁 SAD
- ☐ 😠 MAD

ONE WORD I WOULD USE TO DESCRIBE TODAY:

_____

ONE THING THAT MADE ME HAPPY TODAY:

_____
_____
_____
_____
_____
_____
_____
_____
_____

ONE THING THAT MADE ME SAD OR MAD TODAY:

_____
_____
_____
_____
_____
_____
_____
_____
_____

ONE THING I LEARNED TODAY:

_____
_____

TODAY'S DATE: _____

TODAY I AM FEELING:

- ☐ 🙂 HAPPY
- ☐ 😐 JUST OKAY
- ☐ ☹️ SAD
- ☐ 😠 MAD

ONE WORD I WOULD USE TO DESCRIBE TODAY:
_____

ONE THING THAT MADE ME HAPPY TODAY:

ONE THING THAT MADE ME SAD OR MAD TODAY:

ONE THING I LEARNED TODAY:

TODAY'S DATE: _____

TODAY I AM FEELING:

- ☐ 🙂 HAPPY
- ☐ 😐 JUST OKAY
- ☐ ☹️ SAD
- ☐ 😠 MAD

ONE WORD I WOULD USE TO DESCRIBE TODAY:
_____

ONE THING THAT MADE ME HAPPY TODAY:
_____
_____
_____
_____
_____
_____
_____
_____

ONE THING THAT MADE ME SAD OR MAD TODAY:
_____
_____
_____
_____
_____
_____
_____
_____

ONE THING I LEARNED TODAY:
_____
_____
_____

TODAY'S DATE: _____

TODAY I AM FEELING:
- ☐ 🙂 HAPPY
- ☐ 😐 JUST OKAY
- ☐ 🙁 SAD
- ☐ 😠 MAD

ONE WORD I WOULD USE TO DESCRIBE TODAY:
_____

ONE THING THAT MADE ME HAPPY TODAY:
_____
_____
_____
_____
_____
_____
_____
_____

ONE THING THAT MADE ME SAD OR MAD TODAY:
_____
_____
_____
_____
_____
_____
_____
_____

ONE THING I LEARNED TODAY:
_____
_____
_____
_____

TODAY'S DATE: _____

TODAY I AM FEELING:

- ☐ 🙂 HAPPY
- ☐ 😐 JUST OKAY
- ☐ ☹️ SAD
- ☐ 😠 MAD

ONE WORD I WOULD USE TO DESCRIBE TODAY:

_____

ONE THING THAT MADE ME HAPPY TODAY:

_____
_____
_____
_____
_____
_____
_____
_____
_____

ONE THING THAT MADE ME SAD OR MAD TODAY:

_____
_____
_____
_____
_____
_____
_____
_____
_____

ONE THING I LEARNED TODAY:

_____
_____
_____

TODAY'S DATE: _____

TODAY I AM FEELING:

- ☐ 🙂 HAPPY
- ☐ 😐 JUST OKAY
- ☐ ☹️ SAD
- ☐ 😠 MAD

ONE WORD I WOULD USE TO DESCRIBE TODAY:

_____

ONE THING THAT MADE ME HAPPY TODAY:

_____
_____
_____
_____
_____
_____
_____
_____
_____

ONE THING THAT MADE ME SAD OR MAD TODAY:

_____
_____
_____
_____
_____
_____
_____
_____
_____

ONE THING I LEARNED TODAY:

_____
_____
_____

TODAY'S DATE: _____

TODAY I AM FEELING:

- ☐ 😊 HAPPY
- ☐ 😐 JUST OKAY
- ☐ 😞 SAD
- ☐ 😠 MAD

ONE WORD I WOULD USE TO DESCRIBE TODAY:

_____

ONE THING THAT MADE ME HAPPY TODAY:

_____
_____
_____
_____
_____
_____
_____
_____
_____

ONE THING THAT MADE ME SAD OR MAD TODAY:

_____
_____
_____
_____
_____
_____
_____
_____
_____

ONE THING I LEARNED TODAY:

_____
_____

TODAY'S DATE: _____

TODAY I AM FEELING:

- ☐ HAPPY
- ☐ JUST OKAY
- ☐ SAD
- ☐ MAD

ONE WORD I WOULD USE TO DESCRIBE TODAY:

ONE THING THAT MADE ME HAPPY TODAY:

ONE THING THAT MADE ME SAD OR MAD TODAY:

ONE THING I LEARNED TODAY:

TODAY'S DATE: _____

TODAY I AM FEELING:

- ☐ 🙂 HAPPY
- ☐ 😐 JUST OKAY
- ☐ 🙁 SAD
- ☐ 😠 MAD

ONE WORD I WOULD USE TO DESCRIBE TODAY:

_____

ONE THING THAT MADE ME HAPPY TODAY:

_____
_____
_____
_____
_____
_____
_____
_____

ONE THING THAT MADE ME SAD OR MAD TODAY:

_____
_____
_____
_____
_____
_____
_____
_____

ONE THING I LEARNED TODAY:

_____
_____
_____

TODAY'S DATE: _____

TODAY I AM FEELING:

- ☐ 😊 HAPPY
- ☐ 😐 JUST OKAY
- ☐ 🙁 SAD
- ☐ 😠 MAD

ONE WORD I WOULD USE TO DESCRIBE TODAY:

_____

ONE THING THAT MADE ME HAPPY TODAY:

_____
_____
_____
_____
_____
_____
_____
_____

ONE THING THAT MADE ME SAD OR MAD TODAY:

_____
_____
_____
_____
_____
_____
_____
_____

ONE THING I LEARNED TODAY:

_____
_____
_____

TODAY'S DATE: _____

TODAY I AM FEELING:

- ☐ 🙂 HAPPY
- ☐ 😐 JUST OKAY
- ☐ ☹️ SAD
- ☐ 😠 MAD

ONE WORD I WOULD USE TO DESCRIBE TODAY:

_____

ONE THING THAT MADE ME HAPPY TODAY:

_____
_____
_____
_____
_____
_____
_____
_____

ONE THING THAT MADE ME SAD OR MAD TODAY:

_____
_____
_____
_____
_____
_____
_____
_____

ONE THING I LEARNED TODAY:

_____
_____

TODAY'S DATE: _____

TODAY I AM FEELING:
- ☐ 😊 HAPPY
- ☐ 😐 JUST OKAY
- ☐ ☹️ SAD
- ☐ 😠 MAD

ONE WORD I WOULD USE TO DESCRIBE TODAY:
_____

ONE THING THAT MADE ME HAPPY TODAY:
_____
_____
_____
_____
_____
_____
_____
_____

ONE THING THAT MADE ME SAD OR MAD TODAY:
_____
_____
_____
_____
_____
_____
_____
_____

ONE THING I LEARNED TODAY:
_____
_____
_____

TODAY'S DATE: _____

TODAY I AM FEELING:

- ☐ HAPPY
- ☐ JUST OKAY
- ☐ SAD
- ☐ MAD

ONE WORD I WOULD USE TO DESCRIBE TODAY:

_____

ONE THING THAT MADE ME HAPPY TODAY:

_____
_____
_____
_____
_____
_____
_____
_____

ONE THING THAT MADE ME SAD OR MAD TODAY:

_____
_____
_____
_____
_____
_____
_____
_____

ONE THING I LEARNED TODAY:

_____
_____
_____

TODAY'S DATE: _____

TODAY I AM FEELING:

- ☐ 🙂 HAPPY
- ☐ 😐 JUST OKAY
- ☐ 🙁 SAD
- ☐ 😠 MAD

ONE WORD I WOULD USE TO DESCRIBE TODAY:

_____

ONE THING THAT MADE ME HAPPY TODAY:

_____
_____
_____
_____
_____
_____
_____
_____

ONE THING THAT MADE ME SAD OR MAD TODAY:

_____
_____
_____
_____
_____
_____
_____
_____

ONE THING I LEARNED TODAY:

_____
_____
_____
_____

TODAY'S DATE: _____

TODAY I AM FEELING:
- ☐ 🙂 HAPPY
- ☐ 😐 JUST OKAY
- ☐ ☹️ SAD
- ☐ 😠 MAD

ONE WORD I WOULD USE TO DESCRIBE TODAY:

ONE THING THAT MADE ME HAPPY TODAY:

ONE THING THAT MADE ME SAD OR MAD TODAY:

ONE THING I LEARNED TODAY:

TODAY'S DATE: _____

TODAY I AM FEELING:

- ☐ 😊 HAPPY
- ☐ 😐 JUST OKAY
- ☐ ☹️ SAD
- ☐ 😠 MAD

ONE WORD I WOULD USE TO DESCRIBE TODAY:

_____

ONE THING THAT MADE ME HAPPY TODAY:

_____
_____
_____
_____
_____
_____
_____
_____

ONE THING THAT MADE ME SAD OR MAD TODAY:

_____
_____
_____
_____
_____
_____
_____
_____

ONE THING I LEARNED TODAY:

_____
_____
_____

TODAY'S DATE: _____

TODAY I AM FEELING:

- ☐ 😊 HAPPY
- ☐ 😐 JUST OKAY
- ☐ ☹️ SAD
- ☐ 😠 MAD

ONE WORD I WOULD USE TO DESCRIBE TODAY:

_____

ONE THING THAT MADE ME HAPPY TODAY:

_____
_____
_____
_____
_____
_____
_____
_____

ONE THING THAT MADE ME SAD OR MAD TODAY:

_____
_____
_____
_____
_____
_____
_____
_____

ONE THING I LEARNED TODAY:

_____
_____

TODAY'S DATE: _____

TODAY I AM FEELING:
- ☐ 😊 HAPPY
- ☐ 😐 JUST OKAY
- ☐ 🙁 SAD
- ☐ 😠 MAD

ONE WORD I WOULD USE TO DESCRIBE TODAY:
_____

ONE THING THAT MADE ME HAPPY TODAY:
_____
_____
_____
_____
_____
_____
_____
_____

ONE THING THAT MADE ME SAD OR MAD TODAY:
_____
_____
_____
_____
_____
_____
_____
_____

ONE THING I LEARNED TODAY:
_____
_____
_____

TODAY'S DATE: _____

TODAY I AM FEELING:

- ☐ 🙂 HAPPY
- ☐ 😐 JUST OKAY
- ☐ 🙁 SAD
- ☐ 😠 MAD

ONE WORD I WOULD USE TO DESCRIBE TODAY:

_____

ONE THING THAT MADE ME HAPPY TODAY:

_____

ONE THING THAT MADE ME SAD OR MAD TODAY:

_____

ONE THING I LEARNED TODAY:

_____

TODAY'S DATE: _____

TODAY I AM FEELING:

- ☐ 😊 HAPPY
- ☐ 😐 JUST OKAY
- ☐ 🙁 SAD
- ☐ 😠 MAD

ONE WORD I WOULD USE TO DESCRIBE TODAY:

ONE THING THAT MADE ME HAPPY TODAY:

ONE THING THAT MADE ME SAD OR MAD TODAY:

ONE THING I LEARNED TODAY:

TODAY'S DATE: _____

TODAY I AM FEELING:

- ☐ 🙂 HAPPY
- ☐ 😐 JUST OKAY
- ☐ 🙁 SAD
- ☐ 😠 MAD

ONE WORD I WOULD USE TO DESCRIBE TODAY:

_____

ONE THING THAT MADE ME HAPPY TODAY:

_____
_____
_____
_____
_____
_____
_____
_____
_____

ONE THING THAT MADE ME SAD OR MAD TODAY:

_____
_____
_____
_____
_____
_____
_____
_____
_____

ONE THING I LEARNED TODAY:

_____
_____

TODAY'S DATE: _____

TODAY I AM FEELING:

- ☐ 🙂 HAPPY
- ☐ 😐 JUST OKAY
- ☐ 🙁 SAD
- ☐ 😠 MAD

ONE WORD I WOULD USE TO DESCRIBE TODAY:
_____

ONE THING THAT MADE ME HAPPY TODAY:
_____
_____
_____
_____
_____
_____
_____
_____
_____

ONE THING THAT MADE ME SAD OR MAD TODAY:
_____
_____
_____
_____
_____
_____
_____
_____
_____

ONE THING I LEARNED TODAY:
_____
_____
_____

TODAY'S DATE: _____

TODAY I AM FEELING:

☐ 😊 HAPPY
☐ 😐 JUST OKAY
☐ ☹️ SAD
☐ 😠 MAD

ONE WORD I WOULD USE TO DESCRIBE TODAY:

_____

ONE THING THAT MADE ME HAPPY TODAY:

_____
_____
_____
_____
_____
_____
_____
_____
_____
_____

ONE THING THAT MADE ME SAD OR MAD TODAY:

_____
_____
_____
_____
_____
_____
_____
_____
_____
_____

ONE THING I LEARNED TODAY:

_____
_____
_____

TODAY'S DATE: _____

TODAY I AM FEELING:
- ☐ 🙂 HAPPY
- ☐ 😐 JUST OKAY
- ☐ ☹️ SAD
- ☐ 😠 MAD

ONE WORD I WOULD USE TO DESCRIBE TODAY:
_____

ONE THING THAT MADE ME HAPPY TODAY:
_____
_____
_____
_____
_____
_____
_____
_____

ONE THING THAT MADE ME SAD OR MAD TODAY:
_____
_____
_____
_____
_____
_____
_____
_____

ONE THING I LEARNED TODAY:
_____
_____
_____
_____

TODAY'S DATE: _____

TODAY I AM FEELING:

- ☐ 🙂 HAPPY
- ☐ 😐 JUST OKAY
- ☐ ☹️ SAD
- ☐ 😠 MAD

ONE WORD I WOULD USE TO DESCRIBE TODAY:

ONE THING THAT MADE ME HAPPY TODAY:

ONE THING THAT MADE ME SAD OR MAD TODAY:

ONE THING I LEARNED TODAY:

TODAY'S DATE: _____

TODAY I AM FEELING:

- ☐ 😊 HAPPY
- ☐ 😐 JUST OKAY
- ☐ 🙁 SAD
- ☐ 😠 MAD

ONE WORD I WOULD USE TO DESCRIBE TODAY:

_____

ONE THING THAT MADE ME HAPPY TODAY:

_____
_____
_____
_____
_____
_____
_____
_____

ONE THING THAT MADE ME SAD OR MAD TODAY:

_____
_____
_____
_____
_____
_____
_____
_____

ONE THING I LEARNED TODAY:

_____
_____
_____

TODAY'S DATE: _____

TODAY I AM FEELING:

- ☐ 😊 HAPPY
- ☐ 😐 JUST OKAY
- ☐ ☹️ SAD
- ☐ 😠 MAD

ONE WORD I WOULD USE TO DESCRIBE TODAY:

_____

ONE THING THAT MADE ME HAPPY TODAY:

_____
_____
_____
_____
_____
_____
_____
_____
_____

ONE THING THAT MADE ME SAD OR MAD TODAY:

_____
_____
_____
_____
_____
_____
_____
_____
_____

ONE THING I LEARNED TODAY:

_____
_____
_____

TODAY'S DATE: _____

TODAY I AM FEELING:
- ☐ 😊 HAPPY
- ☐ 😐 JUST OKAY
- ☐ ☹️ SAD
- ☐ 😠 MAD

ONE WORD I WOULD USE TO DESCRIBE TODAY:

ONE THING THAT MADE ME HAPPY TODAY:

ONE THING THAT MADE ME SAD OR MAD TODAY:

ONE THING I LEARNED TODAY:

TODAY'S DATE: _____

TODAY I AM FEELING:

- [ ] 😊 HAPPY
- [ ] 😐 JUST OKAY
- [ ] ☹️ SAD
- [ ] 😠 MAD

ONE WORD I WOULD USE TO DESCRIBE TODAY:
_____

ONE THING THAT MADE ME HAPPY TODAY:
_____
_____
_____
_____
_____
_____
_____
_____

ONE THING THAT MADE ME SAD OR MAD TODAY:
_____
_____
_____
_____
_____
_____
_____
_____

ONE THING I LEARNED TODAY:
_____
_____
_____
_____

TODAY'S DATE: _____

TODAY I AM FEELING:
- ☐ 🙂 HAPPY
- ☐ 😐 JUST OKAY
- ☐ ☹️ SAD
- ☐ 😠 MAD

ONE WORD I WOULD USE TO DESCRIBE TODAY:
_____

ONE THING THAT MADE ME HAPPY TODAY:
_____
_____
_____
_____
_____
_____
_____
_____

ONE THING THAT MADE ME SAD OR MAD TODAY:
_____
_____
_____
_____
_____
_____
_____
_____

ONE THING I LEARNED TODAY:
_____
_____
_____

TODAY'S DATE: _____

TODAY I AM FEELING:

- ☐ 🙂 HAPPY
- ☐ 😐 JUST OKAY
- ☐ ☹️ SAD
- ☐ 😠 MAD

ONE WORD I WOULD USE TO DESCRIBE TODAY:

_____

ONE THING THAT MADE ME HAPPY TODAY:

_____

ONE THING THAT MADE ME SAD OR MAD TODAY:

_____

ONE THING I LEARNED TODAY:

_____

TODAY'S DATE: _____

TODAY I AM FEELING:
- ☐ HAPPY
- ☐ JUST OKAY
- ☐ SAD
- ☐ MAD

ONE WORD I WOULD USE TO DESCRIBE TODAY:

ONE THING THAT MADE ME HAPPY TODAY:

ONE THING THAT MADE ME SAD OR MAD TODAY:

ONE THING I LEARNED TODAY:

TODAY'S DATE: _____

TODAY I AM FEELING:

- ☐ 🙂 HAPPY
- ☐ 😐 JUST OKAY
- ☐ ☹️ SAD
- ☐ 😠 MAD

ONE WORD I WOULD USE TO DESCRIBE TODAY:

_____

ONE THING THAT MADE ME HAPPY TODAY:

_____
_____
_____
_____
_____
_____
_____
_____

ONE THING THAT MADE ME SAD OR MAD TODAY:

_____
_____
_____
_____
_____
_____
_____
_____

ONE THING I LEARNED TODAY:

_____
_____

TODAY'S DATE: _____

TODAY I AM FEELING:

- ☐ 🙂 HAPPY
- ☐ 😐 JUST OKAY
- ☐ 🙁 SAD
- ☐ 😠 MAD

ONE WORD I WOULD USE TO DESCRIBE TODAY:

ONE THING THAT MADE ME HAPPY TODAY:

ONE THING THAT MADE ME SAD OR MAD TODAY:

ONE THING I LEARNED TODAY:

TODAY'S DATE: _____

TODAY I AM FEELING:
- ☐ 🙂 HAPPY
- ☐ 😐 JUST OKAY
- ☐ ☹️ SAD
- ☐ 😠 MAD

ONE WORD I WOULD USE TO DESCRIBE TODAY:

ONE THING THAT MADE ME HAPPY TODAY:

ONE THING THAT MADE ME SAD OR MAD TODAY:

ONE THING I LEARNED TODAY:

TODAY'S DATE: _____

TODAY I AM FEELING:

- ☐ 😊 HAPPY
- ☐ 😐 JUST OKAY
- ☐ 🙁 SAD
- ☐ 😠 MAD

ONE WORD I WOULD USE TO DESCRIBE TODAY:

_____

ONE THING THAT MADE ME HAPPY TODAY:

_____
_____
_____
_____
_____
_____
_____
_____

ONE THING THAT MADE ME SAD OR MAD TODAY:

_____
_____
_____
_____
_____
_____
_____
_____

ONE THING I LEARNED TODAY:

_____
_____
_____

TODAY'S DATE: _____

TODAY I AM FEELING:

- ☐ 🙂 HAPPY
- ☐ 😐 JUST OKAY
- ☐ 🙁 SAD
- ☐ 😠 MAD

ONE WORD I WOULD USE TO DESCRIBE TODAY:
_____

ONE THING THAT MADE ME HAPPY TODAY:
_____
_____
_____
_____
_____
_____
_____
_____
_____

ONE THING THAT MADE ME SAD OR MAD TODAY:
_____
_____
_____
_____
_____
_____
_____
_____
_____

ONE THING I LEARNED TODAY:
_____
_____
_____

TODAY'S DATE: _____

TODAY I AM FEELING:
- ☐ HAPPY
- ☐ JUST OKAY
- ☐ SAD
- ☐ MAD

ONE WORD I WOULD USE TO DESCRIBE TODAY:

_____

ONE THING THAT MADE ME HAPPY TODAY:

_____
_____
_____
_____
_____
_____
_____
_____

ONE THING THAT MADE ME SAD OR MAD TODAY:

_____
_____
_____
_____
_____
_____
_____
_____

ONE THING I LEARNED TODAY:

_____
_____
_____
_____

TODAY'S DATE: _____

TODAY I AM FEELING:
- ☐ 🙂 HAPPY
- ☐ 😐 JUST OKAY
- ☐ 🙁 SAD
- ☐ 😠 MAD

ONE WORD I WOULD USE TO DESCRIBE TODAY:
_____

ONE THING THAT MADE ME HAPPY TODAY:
_____
_____
_____
_____
_____
_____
_____
_____

ONE THING THAT MADE ME SAD OR MAD TODAY:
_____
_____
_____
_____
_____
_____
_____
_____

ONE THING I LEARNED TODAY:
_____
_____
_____

TODAY'S DATE: _____

TODAY I AM FEELING:

- ☐ 🙂 HAPPY
- ☐ 😐 JUST OKAY
- ☐ ☹️ SAD
- ☐ 😠 MAD

ONE WORD I WOULD USE TO DESCRIBE TODAY:

_____

ONE THING THAT MADE ME HAPPY TODAY:

_____
_____
_____
_____
_____
_____
_____
_____

ONE THING THAT MADE ME SAD OR MAD TODAY:

_____
_____
_____
_____
_____
_____
_____
_____

ONE THING I LEARNED TODAY:

_____
_____

TODAY'S DATE: _____

TODAY I AM FEELING:

- ☐ 😊 HAPPY
- ☐ 😐 JUST OKAY
- ☐ ☹️ SAD
- ☐ 😠 MAD

ONE WORD I WOULD USE TO DESCRIBE TODAY:
_____

ONE THING THAT MADE ME HAPPY TODAY:
_____
_____
_____
_____
_____
_____
_____
_____

ONE THING THAT MADE ME SAD OR MAD TODAY:
_____
_____
_____
_____
_____
_____
_____
_____

ONE THING I LEARNED TODAY:
_____
_____
_____

TODAY'S DATE: _____

TODAY I AM FEELING:

- ☐ HAPPY
- ☐ JUST OKAY
- ☐ SAD
- ☐ MAD

ONE WORD I WOULD USE TO DESCRIBE TODAY:
_____

ONE THING THAT MADE ME HAPPY TODAY:
_____
_____
_____
_____
_____
_____
_____
_____

ONE THING THAT MADE ME SAD OR MAD TODAY:
_____
_____
_____
_____
_____
_____
_____
_____

ONE THING I LEARNED TODAY:
_____
_____
_____

TODAY'S DATE: _____

TODAY I AM FEELING:

- ☐ 😊 HAPPY
- ☐ 😐 JUST OKAY
- ☐ ☹️ SAD
- ☐ 😠 MAD

ONE WORD I WOULD USE TO DESCRIBE TODAY:

_____

ONE THING THAT MADE ME HAPPY TODAY:

_____
_____
_____
_____
_____
_____
_____
_____

ONE THING THAT MADE ME SAD OR MAD TODAY:

_____
_____
_____
_____
_____
_____
_____
_____

ONE THING I LEARNED TODAY:

_____
_____
_____
_____

TODAY'S DATE: _____

TODAY I AM FEELING:

- ☐ 🙂 HAPPY
- ☐ 😐 JUST OKAY
- ☐ ☹️ SAD
- ☐ 😠 MAD

ONE WORD I WOULD USE TO DESCRIBE TODAY:

_____

ONE THING THAT MADE ME HAPPY TODAY:

_____
_____
_____
_____
_____
_____
_____
_____
_____
_____

ONE THING THAT MADE ME SAD OR MAD TODAY:

_____
_____
_____
_____
_____
_____
_____
_____
_____
_____

ONE THING I LEARNED TODAY:

_____
_____

TODAY'S DATE: _____

TODAY I AM FEELING:
- ☐ 😊 HAPPY
- ☐ 😐 JUST OKAY
- ☐ ☹️ SAD
- ☐ 😠 MAD

ONE WORD I WOULD USE TO DESCRIBE TODAY:

_____

ONE THING THAT MADE ME HAPPY TODAY:

_____
_____
_____
_____
_____
_____
_____
_____

ONE THING THAT MADE ME SAD OR MAD TODAY:

_____
_____
_____
_____
_____
_____
_____
_____

ONE THING I LEARNED TODAY:

_____
_____
_____

TODAY'S DATE: _____

TODAY I AM FEELING:

- ☐ 🙂 HAPPY
- ☐ 😐 JUST OKAY
- ☐ ☹️ SAD
- ☐ 😠 MAD

ONE WORD I WOULD USE TO DESCRIBE TODAY:
_____

ONE THING THAT MADE ME HAPPY TODAY:
_____
_____
_____
_____
_____
_____
_____
_____

ONE THING THAT MADE ME SAD OR MAD TODAY:
_____
_____
_____
_____
_____
_____
_____
_____

ONE THING I LEARNED TODAY:
_____
_____
_____

TODAY'S DATE: _____

TODAY I AM FEELING:
- ☐ 😊 HAPPY
- ☐ 😐 JUST OKAY
- ☐ ☹️ SAD
- ☐ 😠 MAD

ONE WORD I WOULD USE TO DESCRIBE TODAY:
_____

ONE THING THAT MADE ME HAPPY TODAY:
_____
_____
_____
_____
_____
_____
_____
_____

ONE THING THAT MADE ME SAD OR MAD TODAY:
_____
_____
_____
_____
_____
_____
_____
_____

ONE THING I LEARNED TODAY:
_____
_____
_____

TODAY'S DATE: _____

TODAY I AM FEELING:

- ☐ 🙂 HAPPY
- ☐ 😐 JUST OKAY
- ☐ ☹️ SAD
- ☐ 😠 MAD

ONE WORD I WOULD USE TO DESCRIBE TODAY:

ONE THING THAT MADE ME HAPPY TODAY:

ONE THING THAT MADE ME SAD OR MAD TODAY:

ONE THING I LEARNED TODAY:

TODAY'S DATE: _____

TODAY I AM FEELING:

- ☐ 😊 HAPPY
- ☐ 😐 JUST OKAY
- ☐ 🙁 SAD
- ☐ 😠 MAD

ONE WORD I WOULD USE TO DESCRIBE TODAY:
_____

ONE THING THAT MADE ME HAPPY TODAY:
_____
_____
_____
_____
_____
_____
_____
_____

ONE THING THAT MADE ME SAD OR MAD TODAY:
_____
_____
_____
_____
_____
_____
_____
_____

ONE THING I LEARNED TODAY:
_____
_____
_____

TODAY'S DATE: _____

TODAY I AM FEELING:

- ☐ 🙂 HAPPY
- ☐ 😐 JUST OKAY
- ☐ ☹️ SAD
- ☐ 😠 MAD

ONE WORD I WOULD USE TO DESCRIBE TODAY:

_____

ONE THING THAT MADE ME HAPPY TODAY:

_____
_____
_____
_____
_____
_____
_____
_____
_____

ONE THING THAT MADE ME SAD OR MAD TODAY:

_____
_____
_____
_____
_____
_____
_____
_____
_____

ONE THING I LEARNED TODAY:

_____
_____
_____

TODAY'S DATE: _____

TODAY I AM FEELING:

- ☐ 😊 HAPPY
- ☐ 😐 JUST OKAY
- ☐ 🙁 SAD
- ☐ 😠 MAD

ONE WORD I WOULD USE TO DESCRIBE TODAY:

_____

ONE THING THAT MADE ME HAPPY TODAY:

_____
_____
_____
_____
_____
_____
_____
_____
_____

ONE THING THAT MADE ME SAD OR MAD TODAY:

_____
_____
_____
_____
_____
_____
_____
_____
_____

ONE THING I LEARNED TODAY:

_____
_____
_____

TODAY'S DATE: _____

TODAY I AM FEELING:

- ☐ 🙂 HAPPY
- ☐ 😐 JUST OKAY
- ☐ ☹️ SAD
- ☐ 😠 MAD

ONE WORD I WOULD USE TO DESCRIBE TODAY:
_____

ONE THING THAT MADE ME HAPPY TODAY:
_____
_____
_____
_____
_____
_____
_____
_____
_____

ONE THING THAT MADE ME SAD OR MAD TODAY:
_____
_____
_____
_____
_____
_____
_____
_____
_____

ONE THING I LEARNED TODAY:
_____
_____
_____

TODAY'S DATE: _____

TODAY I AM FEELING:
- ☐ 😊 HAPPY
- ☐ 😐 JUST OKAY
- ☐ ☹️ SAD
- ☐ 😠 MAD

ONE WORD I WOULD USE TO DESCRIBE TODAY:
_____

ONE THING THAT MADE ME HAPPY TODAY:
_____
_____
_____
_____
_____
_____
_____
_____

ONE THING THAT MADE ME SAD OR MAD TODAY:
_____
_____
_____
_____
_____
_____
_____
_____

ONE THING I LEARNED TODAY:
_____
_____
_____

TODAY'S DATE: _____

TODAY I AM FEELING:

- ☐ 🙂 HAPPY
- ☐ 😐 JUST OKAY
- ☐ ☹️ SAD
- ☐ 😠 MAD

ONE WORD I WOULD USE TO DESCRIBE TODAY:
_____

ONE THING THAT MADE ME HAPPY TODAY:

ONE THING THAT MADE ME SAD OR MAD TODAY:

ONE THING I LEARNED TODAY:

TODAY'S DATE: _____

TODAY I AM FEELING:
- ☐ 😊 HAPPY
- ☐ 😐 JUST OKAY
- ☐ 🙁 SAD
- ☐ 😠 MAD

ONE WORD I WOULD USE TO DESCRIBE TODAY:
_____

ONE THING THAT MADE ME HAPPY TODAY:
_____
_____
_____
_____
_____
_____
_____
_____

ONE THING THAT MADE ME SAD OR MAD TODAY:
_____
_____
_____
_____
_____
_____
_____
_____

ONE THING I LEARNED TODAY:
_____
_____
_____

TODAY'S DATE: _____

TODAY I AM FEELING:

- ☐ 🙂 HAPPY
- ☐ 😐 JUST OKAY
- ☐ ☹️ SAD
- ☐ 😠 MAD

ONE WORD I WOULD USE TO DESCRIBE TODAY:
_____

ONE THING THAT MADE ME HAPPY TODAY:

_____
_____
_____
_____
_____
_____
_____
_____
_____

ONE THING THAT MADE ME SAD OR MAD TODAY:

_____
_____
_____
_____
_____
_____
_____
_____
_____

ONE THING I LEARNED TODAY:

_____
_____

TODAY'S DATE: _____

TODAY I AM FEELING:
- ☐ 😊 HAPPY
- ☐ 😐 JUST OKAY
- ☐ ☹️ SAD
- ☐ 😠 MAD

ONE WORD I WOULD USE TO DESCRIBE TODAY:

_____

ONE THING THAT MADE ME HAPPY TODAY:

_____
_____
_____
_____
_____
_____
_____
_____

ONE THING THAT MADE ME SAD OR MAD TODAY:

_____
_____
_____
_____
_____
_____
_____
_____

ONE THING I LEARNED TODAY:

_____
_____
_____
_____

TODAY'S DATE: _____

TODAY I AM FEELING:

- ☐ 🙂 HAPPY
- ☐ 😐 JUST OKAY
- ☐ ☹️ SAD
- ☐ 😠 MAD

ONE WORD I WOULD USE TO DESCRIBE TODAY:

_____

ONE THING THAT MADE ME HAPPY TODAY:

_____
_____
_____
_____
_____
_____
_____
_____

ONE THING THAT MADE ME SAD OR MAD TODAY:

_____
_____
_____
_____
_____
_____
_____
_____

ONE THING I LEARNED TODAY:

_____
_____
_____
_____

TODAY'S DATE: _____

TODAY I AM FEELING:
- ☐ 😊 HAPPY
- ☐ 😐 JUST OKAY
- ☐ ☹️ SAD
- ☐ 😠 MAD

ONE WORD I WOULD USE TO DESCRIBE TODAY:
_____

ONE THING THAT MADE ME HAPPY TODAY:
_____
_____
_____
_____
_____
_____
_____
_____
_____

ONE THING THAT MADE ME SAD OR MAD TODAY:
_____
_____
_____
_____
_____
_____
_____
_____
_____

ONE THING I LEARNED TODAY:
_____
_____
_____

TODAY'S DATE: _____

TODAY I AM FEELING:

- ☐ 🙂 HAPPY
- ☐ 😐 JUST OKAY
- ☐ ☹️ SAD
- ☐ 😠 MAD

ONE WORD I WOULD USE TO DESCRIBE TODAY:

_____

ONE THING THAT MADE ME HAPPY TODAY:

_____
_____
_____
_____
_____
_____
_____
_____

ONE THING THAT MADE ME SAD OR MAD TODAY:

_____
_____
_____
_____
_____
_____
_____
_____

ONE THING I LEARNED TODAY:

_____
_____

TODAY'S DATE: _____

TODAY I AM FEELING:

- ☐ 🙂 HAPPY
- ☐ 😐 JUST OKAY
- ☐ 🙁 SAD
- ☐ 😠 MAD

ONE WORD I WOULD USE TO DESCRIBE TODAY:
_____

ONE THING THAT MADE ME HAPPY TODAY:
_____
_____
_____
_____
_____
_____
_____
_____

ONE THING THAT MADE ME SAD OR MAD TODAY:
_____
_____
_____
_____
_____
_____
_____
_____

ONE THING I LEARNED TODAY:
_____
_____
_____

TODAY'S DATE: _____

TODAY I AM FEELING:

- ☐ 🙂 HAPPY
- ☐ 😐 JUST OKAY
- ☐ ☹️ SAD
- ☐ 😠 MAD

ONE WORD I WOULD USE TO DESCRIBE TODAY:

_____

ONE THING THAT MADE ME HAPPY TODAY:

_____
_____
_____
_____
_____
_____
_____
_____
_____

ONE THING THAT MADE ME SAD OR MAD TODAY:

_____
_____
_____
_____
_____
_____
_____
_____
_____

ONE THING I LEARNED TODAY:

_____
_____
_____

TODAY'S DATE: _____

TODAY I AM FEELING:

- ☐ 🙂 HAPPY
- ☐ 😐 JUST OKAY
- ☐ 🙁 SAD
- ☐ 😠 MAD

ONE WORD I WOULD USE TO DESCRIBE TODAY:

ONE THING THAT MADE ME HAPPY TODAY:

ONE THING THAT MADE ME SAD OR MAD TODAY:

ONE THING I LEARNED TODAY:

TODAY'S DATE: _____

TODAY I AM FEELING:

- ☐ 🙂 HAPPY
- ☐ 😐 JUST OKAY
- ☐ 🙁 SAD
- ☐ 😠 MAD

ONE WORD I WOULD USE TO DESCRIBE TODAY:

_____

ONE THING THAT MADE ME HAPPY TODAY:

_____
_____
_____
_____
_____
_____
_____
_____

ONE THING THAT MADE ME SAD OR MAD TODAY:

_____
_____
_____
_____
_____
_____
_____
_____

ONE THING I LEARNED TODAY:

_____
_____
_____

TODAY'S DATE: _____

TODAY I AM FEELING:
- ☐ 😊 HAPPY
- ☐ 😐 JUST OKAY
- ☐ ☹️ SAD
- ☐ 😠 MAD

ONE WORD I WOULD USE TO DESCRIBE TODAY:
_____

ONE THING THAT MADE ME HAPPY TODAY:
_____
_____
_____
_____
_____
_____
_____
_____

ONE THING THAT MADE ME SAD OR MAD TODAY:
_____
_____
_____
_____
_____
_____
_____
_____

ONE THING I LEARNED TODAY:
_____
_____
_____

TODAY'S DATE: _____

TODAY I AM FEELING:

- ☐ 🙂 HAPPY
- ☐ 😐 JUST OKAY
- ☐ 🙁 SAD
- ☐ 😠 MAD

ONE WORD I WOULD USE TO DESCRIBE TODAY:
_____

ONE THING THAT MADE ME HAPPY TODAY:

ONE THING THAT MADE ME SAD OR MAD TODAY:

ONE THING I LEARNED TODAY:

TODAY'S DATE: _____

TODAY I AM FEELING:
- [ ] HAPPY
- [ ] JUST OKAY
- [ ] SAD
- [ ] MAD

ONE WORD I WOULD USE TO DESCRIBE TODAY:

ONE THING THAT MADE ME HAPPY TODAY:

ONE THING THAT MADE ME SAD OR MAD TODAY:

ONE THING I LEARNED TODAY:

TODAY'S DATE: _____

TODAY I AM FEELING:

- ☐ 🙂 HAPPY
- ☐ 😐 JUST OKAY
- ☐ ☹️ SAD
- ☐ 😠 MAD

ONE WORD I WOULD USE TO DESCRIBE TODAY:

ONE THING THAT MADE ME HAPPY TODAY:

ONE THING THAT MADE ME SAD OR MAD TODAY:

ONE THING I LEARNED TODAY:

TODAY'S DATE: _____

TODAY I AM FEELING:

- ☐ 😊 HAPPY
- ☐ 😐 JUST OKAY
- ☐ ☹️ SAD
- ☐ 😠 MAD

ONE WORD I WOULD USE TO DESCRIBE TODAY:

_____

ONE THING THAT MADE ME HAPPY TODAY:

_____
_____
_____
_____
_____
_____
_____
_____

ONE THING THAT MADE ME SAD OR MAD TODAY:

_____
_____
_____
_____
_____
_____
_____
_____

ONE THING I LEARNED TODAY:

_____
_____
_____

TODAY'S DATE: _____

TODAY I AM FEELING:

- ☐ 🙂 HAPPY
- ☐ 😐 JUST OKAY
- ☐ ☹️ SAD
- ☐ 😠 MAD

ONE WORD I WOULD USE TO DESCRIBE TODAY:

_____

ONE THING THAT MADE ME HAPPY TODAY:

_____
_____
_____
_____
_____
_____
_____
_____
_____

ONE THING THAT MADE ME SAD OR MAD TODAY:

_____
_____
_____
_____
_____
_____
_____
_____
_____

ONE THING I LEARNED TODAY:

_____
_____

TODAY'S DATE: _____

TODAY I AM FEELING:

- ☐ HAPPY
- ☐ JUST OKAY
- ☐ SAD
- ☐ MAD

ONE WORD I WOULD USE TO DESCRIBE TODAY:
_____

ONE THING THAT MADE ME HAPPY TODAY:

ONE THING THAT MADE ME SAD OR MAD TODAY:

ONE THING I LEARNED TODAY:

TODAY'S DATE: _____

TODAY I AM FEELING:

- ☐ 🙂 HAPPY
- ☐ 😐 JUST OKAY
- ☐ ☹️ SAD
- ☐ 😠 MAD

ONE WORD I WOULD USE TO DESCRIBE TODAY:

_____

ONE THING THAT MADE ME HAPPY TODAY:

_____
_____
_____
_____
_____
_____
_____
_____

ONE THING THAT MADE ME SAD OR MAD TODAY:

_____
_____
_____
_____
_____
_____
_____
_____

ONE THING I LEARNED TODAY:

_____
_____

TODAY'S DATE: _____

TODAY I AM FEELING:

- ☐ 🙂 HAPPY
- ☐ 😐 JUST OKAY
- ☐ 🙁 SAD
- ☐ 😠 MAD

ONE WORD I WOULD USE TO DESCRIBE TODAY:

_____

ONE THING THAT MADE ME HAPPY TODAY:

ONE THING THAT MADE ME SAD OR MAD TODAY:

ONE THING I LEARNED TODAY:

TODAY'S DATE: _____

TODAY I AM FEELING:

- ☐ 🙂 HAPPY
- ☐ 😐 JUST OKAY
- ☐ 🙁 SAD
- ☐ 😠 MAD

ONE WORD I WOULD USE TO DESCRIBE TODAY:

_____

ONE THING THAT MADE ME HAPPY TODAY:

_____
_____
_____
_____
_____
_____
_____
_____

ONE THING THAT MADE ME SAD OR MAD TODAY:

_____
_____
_____
_____
_____
_____
_____
_____

ONE THING I LEARNED TODAY:

_____
_____

TODAY'S DATE: _____

TODAY I AM FEELING:

- ☐ 😊 HAPPY
- ☐ 😐 JUST OKAY
- ☐ ☹️ SAD
- ☐ 😠 MAD

ONE WORD I WOULD USE TO DESCRIBE TODAY:

_____

ONE THING THAT MADE ME HAPPY TODAY:

ONE THING THAT MADE ME SAD OR MAD TODAY:

ONE THING I LEARNED TODAY:

TODAY'S DATE: _____

TODAY I AM FEELING:
- ☐ 🙂 HAPPY
- ☐ 😐 JUST OKAY
- ☐ ☹️ SAD
- ☐ 😠 MAD

ONE WORD I WOULD USE TO DESCRIBE TODAY:
_____

ONE THING THAT MADE ME HAPPY TODAY:
_____
_____
_____
_____
_____
_____
_____
_____

ONE THING THAT MADE ME SAD OR MAD TODAY:
_____
_____
_____
_____
_____
_____
_____
_____

ONE THING I LEARNED TODAY:
_____
_____

TODAY'S DATE: _____

TODAY I AM FEELING:
- ☐ 😊 HAPPY
- ☐ 😐 JUST OKAY
- ☐ ☹️ SAD
- ☐ 😠 MAD

ONE WORD I WOULD USE TO DESCRIBE TODAY:

ONE THING THAT MADE ME HAPPY TODAY:

ONE THING THAT MADE ME SAD OR MAD TODAY:

ONE THING I LEARNED TODAY:

TODAY'S DATE: _____

TODAY I AM FEELING:

- ☐ 😊 HAPPY
- ☐ 😐 JUST OKAY
- ☐ 😢 SAD
- ☐ 😠 MAD

ONE WORD I WOULD USE TO DESCRIBE TODAY:

ONE THING THAT MADE ME HAPPY TODAY:

ONE THING THAT MADE ME SAD OR MAD TODAY:

ONE THING I LEARNED TODAY:

TODAY'S DATE: _____

TODAY I AM FEELING:

- ☐ 😊 HAPPY
- ☐ 😐 JUST OKAY
- ☐ ☹️ SAD
- ☐ 😠 MAD

ONE WORD I WOULD USE TO DESCRIBE TODAY:

ONE THING THAT MADE ME HAPPY TODAY:

ONE THING THAT MADE ME SAD OR MAD TODAY:

ONE THING I LEARNED TODAY:

TODAY'S DATE: _____

TODAY I AM FEELING:

- ☐ 😊 HAPPY
- ☐ 😐 JUST OKAY
- ☐ ☹️ SAD
- ☐ 😠 MAD

ONE WORD I WOULD USE TO DESCRIBE TODAY:

ONE THING THAT MADE ME HAPPY TODAY:

ONE THING THAT MADE ME SAD OR MAD TODAY:

ONE THING I LEARNED TODAY:

TODAY'S DATE: _____

TODAY I AM FEELING:

- ☐ 🙂 HAPPY
- ☐ 😐 JUST OKAY
- ☐ ☹️ SAD
- ☐ 😠 MAD

ONE WORD I WOULD USE TO DESCRIBE TODAY:

_____

ONE THING THAT MADE ME HAPPY TODAY:

_____
_____
_____
_____
_____
_____
_____

ONE THING THAT MADE ME SAD OR MAD TODAY:

_____
_____
_____
_____
_____
_____
_____

ONE THING I LEARNED TODAY:

_____
_____
_____

TODAY'S DATE: _____

TODAY I AM FEELING:

- ☐ 🙂 HAPPY
- ☐ 😐 JUST OKAY
- ☐ ☹️ SAD
- ☐ 😠 MAD

ONE WORD I WOULD USE TO DESCRIBE TODAY:

_____

ONE THING THAT MADE ME HAPPY TODAY:

_____
_____
_____
_____
_____
_____
_____
_____
_____

ONE THING THAT MADE ME SAD OR MAD TODAY:

_____
_____
_____
_____
_____
_____
_____
_____
_____

ONE THING I LEARNED TODAY:

_____
_____
_____

TODAY'S DATE: _____

TODAY I AM FEELING:

- ☐ 😊 HAPPY
- ☐ 😐 JUST OKAY
- ☐ 🙁 SAD
- ☐ 😠 MAD

ONE WORD I WOULD USE TO DESCRIBE TODAY:

_____

ONE THING THAT MADE ME HAPPY TODAY:

_____
_____
_____
_____
_____
_____
_____
_____

ONE THING THAT MADE ME SAD OR MAD TODAY:

_____
_____
_____
_____
_____
_____
_____
_____

ONE THING I LEARNED TODAY:

_____
_____
_____

TODAY'S DATE: _____

TODAY I AM FEELING:

- ☐ 🙂 HAPPY
- ☐ 😐 JUST OKAY
- ☐ 🙁 SAD
- ☐ 😠 MAD

ONE WORD I WOULD USE TO DESCRIBE TODAY:

_____

ONE THING THAT MADE ME HAPPY TODAY:

ONE THING THAT MADE ME SAD OR MAD TODAY:

ONE THING I LEARNED TODAY:

TODAY'S DATE: _____

TODAY I AM FEELING:

- ☐ 🙂 HAPPY
- ☐ 😐 JUST OKAY
- ☐ 🙁 SAD
- ☐ 😠 MAD

ONE WORD I WOULD USE TO DESCRIBE TODAY:

_____

ONE THING THAT MADE ME HAPPY TODAY:

_____
_____
_____
_____
_____
_____
_____
_____

ONE THING THAT MADE ME SAD OR MAD TODAY:

_____
_____
_____
_____
_____
_____
_____
_____

ONE THING I LEARNED TODAY:

_____
_____
_____

TODAY'S DATE: _____

TODAY I AM FEELING:

- ☐ 🙂 HAPPY
- ☐ 😐 JUST OKAY
- ☐ 🙁 SAD
- ☐ 😠 MAD

ONE WORD I WOULD USE TO DESCRIBE TODAY:
_____

ONE THING THAT MADE ME HAPPY TODAY:
_____
_____
_____
_____
_____
_____
_____
_____
_____

ONE THING THAT MADE ME SAD OR MAD TODAY:
_____
_____
_____
_____
_____
_____
_____
_____
_____

ONE THING I LEARNED TODAY:
_____
_____

TODAY'S DATE: _____

TODAY I AM FEELING:
- ☐ HAPPY
- ☐ JUST OKAY
- ☐ SAD
- ☐ MAD

ONE WORD I WOULD USE TO DESCRIBE TODAY:

ONE THING THAT MADE ME HAPPY TODAY:

ONE THING THAT MADE ME SAD OR MAD TODAY:

ONE THING I LEARNED TODAY:

TODAY'S DATE: _____

TODAY I AM FEELING:

- ☐ 🙂 HAPPY
- ☐ 😐 JUST OKAY
- ☐ ☹️ SAD
- ☐ 😠 MAD

ONE WORD I WOULD USE TO DESCRIBE TODAY:

_____

ONE THING THAT MADE ME HAPPY TODAY:

_____
_____
_____
_____
_____
_____
_____
_____
_____

ONE THING THAT MADE ME SAD OR MAD TODAY:

_____
_____
_____
_____
_____
_____
_____
_____
_____

ONE THING I LEARNED TODAY:

_____
_____
_____
_____

TODAY'S DATE: _____

TODAY I AM FEELING:

- ☐ 😊 HAPPY
- ☐ 😐 JUST OKAY
- ☐ ☹️ SAD
- ☐ 😠 MAD

ONE WORD I WOULD USE TO DESCRIBE TODAY:
_____

ONE THING THAT MADE ME HAPPY TODAY:
_____
_____
_____
_____
_____
_____
_____
_____

ONE THING THAT MADE ME SAD OR MAD TODAY:
_____
_____
_____
_____
_____
_____
_____
_____

ONE THING I LEARNED TODAY:
_____
_____
_____

TODAY'S DATE: _____

TODAY I AM FEELING:

- ☐ 🙂 HAPPY
- ☐ 😐 JUST OKAY
- ☐ 🙁 SAD
- ☐ 😠 MAD

ONE WORD I WOULD USE TO DESCRIBE TODAY:

_____

ONE THING THAT MADE ME HAPPY TODAY:

_____
_____
_____
_____
_____
_____
_____
_____

ONE THING THAT MADE ME SAD OR MAD TODAY:

_____
_____
_____
_____
_____
_____
_____
_____

ONE THING I LEARNED TODAY:

_____
_____

TODAY'S DATE: _____

TODAY I AM FEELING:
- ☐ 😊 HAPPY
- ☐ 😐 JUST OKAY
- ☐ 🙁 SAD
- ☐ 😠 MAD

ONE WORD I WOULD USE TO DESCRIBE TODAY:
_____

ONE THING THAT MADE ME HAPPY TODAY:
_____
_____
_____
_____
_____
_____
_____
_____

ONE THING THAT MADE ME SAD OR MAD TODAY:
_____
_____
_____
_____
_____
_____
_____
_____

ONE THING I LEARNED TODAY:
_____
_____
_____

TODAY'S DATE: _____

TODAY I AM FEELING:

☐ 🙂 HAPPY
☐ 😐 JUST OKAY
☐ ☹️ SAD
☐ 😠 MAD

ONE WORD I WOULD USE TO DESCRIBE TODAY:
_____

ONE THING THAT MADE ME HAPPY TODAY:
_____
_____
_____
_____
_____
_____
_____
_____
_____

ONE THING THAT MADE ME SAD OR MAD TODAY:
_____
_____
_____
_____
_____
_____
_____
_____
_____

ONE THING I LEARNED TODAY:
_____
_____
_____

Made in United States
Troutdale, OR
04/16/2024